Images of War
THE RED ARMY AT WAR

Images of War
THE RED ARMY AT WAR

RARE PHOTOGRAPHS FROM WARTIME ARCHIVES

Artem Drabkin

Translated by Vladimir Kroupnik
English text by Christopher Summerville

Pen & Sword
MILITARY

First published in Great Britain in 2010 by
Pen & Sword Military
an imprint of
Pen & Sword Books Ltd
47 Church Street, Barnsley
South Yorkshire
S70 2AS

Photographs provided by the Russian State Documentary Film and Photograph Archive, the Artem Drabkin Archive and the archive of the Veterans' Committee of the Karelian Front.

ISBN 9781848840553

Typeset in 12pt GillSans Light by Pen & Sword Books Ltd., Barnsley

Printed and bound in Great Britain by CPI

Pen & Sword Books Ltd incorporates the imprints of Pen & Sword Aviation, Pen & Sword Maritime, Pen & Sword Military, Wharncliffe Local History, Pen and Sword Select, Pen and Sword Military Classics, Leo Cooper, Remember When, Seaforth Publishing and Frontline Publishing.

For a complete list of Pen & Sword titles please contact
PEN & SWORD BOOKS LIMITED
47 Church Street, Barnsley, South Yorkshire, S70 2AS, England
E-mail: enquiries@pen-and-sword.co.uk
Website: www.pen-and-sword.co.uk

Contents

Chapter 1
Drafting

Before 1938 up to 80 per cent of Red Army units were formed on the territorial-militia basis. Menfolk capable of carrying arms were drafted for a limited period into territorial units, which made up about a half of the Army. The first service term was three months in a year, followed by one month annually during a five-year period. The regular, non-territorial, half of the Army was formed by drafting, with a service term of two years. Later, the territorial system was abolished and militia units were run on the same lines as the regulars.

Men who had reached the age of 18 were subject to drafting into military service. And young men who had completed no less than seven years of school could join military academies, which trained commanders for land troops. The educational qualification for aviation academies was higher: nine years of school education. One would have to pass exams and be tested by a medical board. Finally, would-be recruits were scrutinized by a credentials committee, which checked family records for political and ideological suitability.

Volunteers registering for military service at an enlistment office during the first days of the war. The man in uniform is an orderly: he either considers applications for enlistment or accepts call-up papers from conscripts. The man with a telephone receiver in his hand apparently reports to his superiors on the attendance of volunteers and conscripts. The patriotic impulse was initially so great that military registration and enlistment offices couldn't cope with the enormous influx of volunteers. However, by autumn of 1941 this stream had dried up because of the protracted war and early Russian defeats.

Army service was prestigious, for it provided a higher standard of living than civilian life, as well as the opportunity for learning professional skills.

Total mobilization was declared in the USSR with the outbreak of war. The first wave (young men born between 1918 and 1923) occurred in the summer of 1941. Those who worked at military production plants or as harvesters in the countryside were exempt. Dmitry Boulgakov from the Kursk Oblast [i.e. Region – trans.] remembers:

> On the second day after the announcement of the war the conscripts got their call-up papers, with the order to report to the *selsovet* [i.e. village council – trans.]. The whole village was in tears seeing the menfolk marching off to the war. My elder brother – who was a combine harvester operator – would be called up only in July, as at first the combine operators were not to be drafted. In September they announced that all men born between 1890 and 1923 were to be called up, and would be evacuated to the south-east.

Simultaneously, volunteers were enlisted into fighter detachments and people's militia [i.e. paramilitary units similar to the Home Guard in Great Britain – trans.]. Natalia Peshkova remembers:

Young Leningrad workers undergoing military training. The lad with ammo belts round his chest holds the body of a Maxim machine gun. His neighbour on the right holds the weapon shield. The shoulder straps of the soldier in the background date this photo to no earlier than 1943.

Conscripts in the streets of Leningrad, 1941. The windows of the shop selling 'Frukty' ('Fruits') are already sealed up with paper strips.

I had just graduated from school. We had a traditional ceremony and walked around Red Square. The war began next day. Well, I regarded myself as no less than Joan of Arc, so I immediately ran to the district Komsomol [i.e. Young Communists League – trans.] committee and they sent me to a group of medics. This group was based in our school. We learned how to put on bandages and splints, how to give injections, etc. We were even taught to crawl flat on the ground in our school auditorium. At that time the militia units (DNO) were being formed in Moscow. I was sent to a rifle company of a DNO division as a medic.

Ion Degen tells a similar story:

I ran up to the *voenkomat* [i.e. military commissariat – trans.] but no one was going to talk to me anywhere. I was shaking the air with exclamations about the duty of a Komsomol member, defence of the Motherland, heroes of the Civil War. The answer was brief: 'We don't take kids into the Army!' But already on the tenth day of the war a volunteer fighter battalion consisting of Year 9–10 students of the city schools was raised by the Komsomol committee. Our platoon comprised Year 9 students with almost all of them born in 1924, and only three in 1925.

But exemption from service was still preserved at the military production plants. Michael Kuznetsov remembers: 'In the autumn a directive came: all men of such-and-such a year of birth to report to the *voenkomat*. I came up, but it turned out that I was exempt. They demanded my passport from me, but it had been taken away back at the plant and instead I'd been given an identity card with a red star. The *voenkom* [i.e. military commissar – trans.] says: "I can't draft you." I went out and said to the guy I'd come up with: "That's it, I'm not drafted." Lesha Orekhov says: "Goddamn it! Wait for half an hour, then put on my coat and hat, come in and say the plant's gone and you want to join the forces!" So I did and was enlisted.'

People were eager to fight for different reasons: love of the Motherland, revenge for the death of fallen kinfolk, or, as with Nikolay Smol'sky, a sense of duty and honour. Nikolay Smol'sky had graduated from an aviation school and found himself in a Reserve Aviation Regiment, in which, from his view, he might stay till the end of the war:

I began to look for an opportunity to make my way to the front. Back then I was thinking this way: eventually my kids will ask me: 'What did you do, Dad, when everyone fought?' What will I answer them with?

Departure to the front, 1941. They are still alive and they have no medals or orders on their chests. Some have badges, 'Voroshilovsky Strelok' ('Voroshilov's Shooter') and 'Otlichnik RKKA' ('a high achiever of the Red Army'). The military man with papers in his hand is a political instructor. He wears an arm badge in the form of a star. Railway goods vans, commonly known as 'teplushkas' ('warm vans') were a typical means of transport to the front. Every van accommodated 'twenty horses or forty men'.

A grandfather sees his grandson off to the front, 1941. The soldier holds a semi-automatic SVT-40 rifle. This rifle was very expensive to produce, and was deemed too difficult for most technologically illiterate infantrymen to handle, so it was taken out of production. Also visible is a steel helmet of the 1936 pattern and a tarpaulin or kersey waist-belt.

But there was also another reason – hunger. The slogan 'All for the front!' had been put into practice and people at home were starving.

From 1943 the Red Army began liberating vast swathes abandoned during the first months of the war. This territory contained men of call-up age previously untouched by mobilization, juveniles who had reached the age of 18, plus ex-soldiers of the Red Army who had managed to settle down [i.e. in the occupied territories – trans.] and partisans. This motley mass of men would be immediately called up and often thrown into combat before receiving a uniform. Vladimir Boukhenko remembers:

> During the liberation of the Ukraine we were constantly reinforced by local menfolk. Often there was no time to dress them up in military uniform, and because of that they were called 'black shirts'.

Dmitry Boulgakov remembers:

> The HQ of a battalion from the 931st Regiment of the 240th Division was set up in an unburned shack. Drafting of all men born between 1890 and 1924 was announced. There was no medical examination. Nor was there any uniform. But they were given rifles. Two platoons were raised, manned by the locals under the charge of staff commanders. Many of them had never served in the Army and didn't know how to handle firearms. Only two Germans came close to them, shot a burst and yelled 'Hände hoch!' They raised their arms, without having fired a single shot. After all, they had become accustomed to German masters barking orders. All those guys perished except one, who managed to escape and tell the story.

Taking the oath. In the background you can see an Air Force officer, so we can assume the soldiers taking the oath serve in an Airfield Service Battalion. The combination of shoulder straps and turn-down collars dates this photo to 1943.

Chapter 2
Training

A team of draftees would get their papers and head for a training camp, where they would undergo basic military instruction, or, as it was termed back then, 'Young Red Army soldier's course'. The course lasted three months and most veterans recall it with horror. Ilya Sokolov found himself at the Chebarkoul camp in the South Urals:

> A freight train stopped in a pine forest. The snow was knee-deep. A lame *starshina* [i.e. sergeant major – trans.] lined us up and marched us deep inside the forest. After 4 kilometres we saw smoke ahead, coming from dugouts. Each one was intended for 250 men. On both sides of the central passage were double bunks built of unshaved planks. A stove for heating stood at the end of the dugout. No mattresses, blankets or pillows were issued. We broke off brushwood and plaited rags into mattresses to sleep on. I slept on such a bed for three months. Reveille was at six in the morning. We would run out, wash with snow, get a piece of sticky mass called 'bread', and march in formation 5 kilometres to the drill ground with full combat kit (rifle, gas mask, ammo, backpack). They drilled us to shoot, taught us the basics of hand-to-hand and bayonet fighting. Having got fed up with crawling in the snow, we would return to the regiment for lunch. The tucker was disgusting! A bowl of greenish water with a couple of floating

Training for anti-tank warfare, Leningrad 1941. The instructor holds a bundle of four RGD-33 anti-personnel grenades – it was recommended to throw such a bundle under the tracks of German tanks.

cabbage leaves and a ration of raw bread. Sometimes we were given rotten fish with a ladle of *kasha* [i.e. porridge or gruel – trans.] – and that was a feast for us [. . .]. Many guys had weakened so badly on this feed, they were transferred to the 'feeble' battalion, where they were fed up and given a yeast drink. Even sturdy Siberians couldn't cope with the hunger. Local guys began to defect. They would be caught. Every week we'd be lined up by the dugouts for show trials. A travelling court martial would come around and we watched as the deserters from the regiment were sentenced to death and executed on the spot [. . .]. Occasionally, someone was lucky enough to be sent to a penal company instead of getting capital punishment. The three months in the drill regiment seemed like three years [. . .]. At last, at the beginning of June 1943, we had a *banya* [i.e. steam bath – trans.] for the first time and were given a new uniform, plus boots with new puttees. We received backpacks with a flask, mess tin, mug, spoon, and dry rations for three days, which we ate straight away. Then we boarded a train and headed for the front.

An artillery lieutenant of the 23rd Guards Rifle Division (26th Army) trains his men to operate the 50mm company mortar, model 1941.

Training snipers – a portrait of Hitler serves as the target. In the hands of the soldier you can see a Mosin rifle (model 1898/1930) fitted with a 'PE' telescopic sight.

The situation in military schools was noticeably different and officer cadets were better fed. Training lasted twelve hours a day: eight hours of theory and practice plus four hours of independent self-training under the guidance of a teacher. After six months of this accelerated drilling, cadets received the rank of lieutenant or junior lieutenant and were sent to the front. According to Vasily Bryukhov, who graduated from the Stalingrad Tank School in the spring of 1943, the Principal dismissed graduates with the following words: 'Well, boys, we understand that you've run through the programme quickly. You have not perfected your knowledge but you'll finalize it in action.' This approach to training was typical for infantry as well as tank and aviation schools. An airman, Ivan Gaidayenko – who was retrained during the war from an SB bomber pilot into an I-16 fighter pilot – remembers:

> I said to the instructor: 'Show me how to run the dogfight. After all, I'm from a bomber, I've never learned aerobatics.' He says: 'First, aerobatics are banned; second, when you're in a dogfight you have to put your plane into a spin – if you can't do that you'll be downed.'

Experienced commanders used any opportunity – such as a lull between engagements – to increase the skills of their subordinates. A scout, Leonid Knyazik, remembers:

We were taught to crawl noiselessly, to overcome barbed-wire entanglements. We were shown how to 'take out a sentry'. I have to say that, if you were assigned to be a 'German sentry' during drilling, it wasn't a very pleasant experience . . .

Rehearsing an attack – infantrymen follow a T-60 light tank.

An attack in mounted formation – the Red Army used cavalry as mobile infantry.

Rolling by a tank. The crew of a PTRD anti-tank rifle must let the T-34 tank drive over them, before throwing grenades into it.

A lieutenant instructs his men on the construction of the Maxim machine gun.

Study of the British Valentine tank. Often there were no translated instructions for vehicles supplied via Lend-Lease, so soldiers and their commanders had to master them by trial and error.

A sergeant conducts a lesson for making individual rifle trenches. He wears a model 1936 helmet (as does the soldier standing second from the left), the others wear the model 1940.

An experienced pilot – apparently the squadron commander or his deputy – explains the nuances of the Il-2 single-seater ground-attack plane to new pilots (7th Air Army).

Soldiers convalescing from wounds recover physical strength training in hand-to-hand combat. On the horizontal bar of the 'cross' is an inscription: 'Therapeutic physical training is the main method of treatment for the whole organism.'

Chapter 3
Marching

People were transported to the front in freight wagons equipped with bunk beds and small stoves. The trains would stop at stations on the way, to take on hot food. Vasily Bryukhov, who headed to the front in 1944 as a tank platoon commander, recalls:

> We were ordered not to take fellow-travellers onboard, but there were so many willing! Displaced by the war from their old haunts, evacuated many kilometres away from home, they were on their way back. By fair means or foul they would find their way to the open wagons and crawl under the soft covers.

An infantryman, Vladimir Boukhenko, making his way to the front in the summer of 1942, remembers:

> On our way to the front we constantly socialized with wounded men transported to the rear for treatment. From their stories we learned that they'd been in action no more than a month or two. We gradually began to understand that, at best, we'd be in hospital within a couple of months.

Infantry on the march. In front can be seen an S-65 'Stalinets' tractor, which pulls a 76.2mm anti-aircraft gun, model 1930/1931.

It's 20 kilometres to Danzig.

Nevertheless, as a radio operator and machine-gunner of a T-34 tank, Leonid Katz recalled that, even in the darkest days of 1941, 'there was no despair or feeling of being doomed. We were all 20 years old, all patriots brought up by the Soviet system in a fanatical spirit.'

Having detrained, men would march to the muster areas. From the end of 1943, when the Red Army switched to the offensive, marches of many days were a typical part of infantry life. Efim Golbraikh remembers:

> A foot soldier is loaded like a donkey: trench coat, backpack, goddamn gas mask (stuffed with hand grenades), steel helmet, entrenching tool, mess tin, map-case, and several ammo pouches, plus a rifle or submachine-gun. You're sweating all over. White salt stains would appear on your blouse – you'd take it off and it would stand upright on its own. On the march, we were given sunflower seeds by liberated villagers – what the Germans called 'Russian chocolate'. The seeds helped pass time on the road. By the time you'd cracked a full pocket of seeds, 10 kilometres had gone. Such was the soldier's speedometer. I remember 80-kilometre marches as a nightmare. We slept on the way. On top of everything else, they would hang four 82mm mortar shells on each of us. You ain't recommended to fall over with a shell round your neck, especially a second time – one of them might have switched to full cock from the shock [...]. You walk, your whole body itches from sweat and lice, your stomach sticks to your backbone from hunger. Thus we walked our way to Victory ...

Soldiers would fall asleep on their feet, stumble out of formation and tumble into roadside ditches due to exhaustion. As a precaution, they tried to grip the shoulder of the man in front; or they marched three abreast – the man in the middle asleep, supported by comrades on either side, then they would swap over.

A platoon of submachine-gunners on the march.

Life was much harder for the commandos and partisans who operated behind enemy lines. Anna Arkhipova – a two-way radio operator in a partisan detachment – recalls:

We would get 200 kilometres into Finnish territory and even more than that. We walked for eighteen hours during a march. After all, we carried all our supplies – ammo and food – in backpacks, therefore any delay threatened starvation, as we could only carry the bare minimum for survival. Even so, our backs were still cracking [. . .] We walked in silence, three scouts in the vanguard. Combat protection was from both sides. Orders and news were passed along the file. No way could one step out of line under any excuse – even to urinate. That was why, if there was an urge – do it in the pants! All of us girls had cystitis. We didn't wear bras or underwear – we had none. We had no time to think about ourselves! Sure, by the end of a raid, any bear would run a mile from our stink [. . .] Every forty minutes we had a rest. We longed for a stopover like manna from heaven. A stopover lasted ten minutes. You'd lift the backpack with strain, inwardly cursing the war – and sometimes aloud!

Servicemen from mechanized brigades were better off. A sapper, Michael Tsourkan, remembers:

We rarely went by foot during marches. We were transported in the ZIS or *polutorka* [1.5-tonne truck – trans.] trucks, and we were always covered by flak gunners [. . .] I sat on the left side, and when the vehicle began to skid, I would have to jump off and put a special chock under the wheels. And during night marches they would tie me up to the bench, for sometimes the ones sitting on the edge had their heads torn off by oncoming vehicles [. . .] Once, in Romania, our vehicle stopped because a soldier's corpse had stuck between the back wheels and wouldn't let us move . . .

Flights to the front were not much easier for airmen. A Pe-2 pilot, Ivan Kabakov, recalls:

The route from Irkutsk to Leningrad was several times longer than my total flight hours spent in the air in this type of aircraft! We flew over to Kazan using the 'Kaganovich compass' [a joke name for a railroad, named after the People's Commissar of Railroads, L.M. Kaganovich – trans.]. The ground services along this route were very primitive. There were practically no reserve aerodromes, and meteorological services were very weak. During the relocation our regiment lost two planes. One caught fire near Krasnoyarsk. The crew died. Another plane landed in Kansk with retracted landing gear. An Army aviation regiment followed us. And they managed to get to Kazan with only fifteen planes!

It may be said the constant relocation of advancing and retreating troops was a heavy burden for all branches of the Armed Forces.

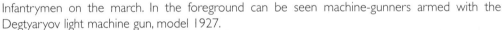

Infantrymen on the march. In the foreground can be seen machine-gunners armed with the Degtyaryov light machine gun, model 1927.

A Maxim machine-gun crew (26th Army) deploys. This machine gun was used by the Red Army throughout the whole war. Although heavy and water-cooled, it was extremely reliable.

Carrying an 82mm mortar, model 1937. The weight of the mortar plate exceeded 20 kilograms. If a soldier fell while carrying it, the weight could easily break his cervical vertebrae.

Two images of forced river crossings, one undertaken by the crew of a 45mm gun.

A long-awaited halt! The soldier in the foreground carries not only his knapsack, but also his gas mask. Soldiers usually discarded their gas masks and heavy anti-tank grenades on the march, filling their bags with extra ammunition or personal belongings.

The crew of a 50mm company mortar. These weapons were widely used by the Red Army at the beginning of the war, but later it was found to be ineffective and was gradually phased out.

A battery of 122mm howitzers on the march. Each gun is pulled by six horses. In front, wearing the Order of the Red Star on his blouse, you can see the battery commander.

The Karelian Front: the crew of a 45mm gun pull their weapon to the top of a cone-shaped hill. A Red Fleet sailor stands out against a background of soldiers. Brigades of infantrymen were often formed from naval personnel, who, believing it beneath their dignity, refused to swap uniforms.

Chapter 4
Entertainment

In spite of all the hardships of front-line life, people remained people, and during their leisure time tried to divert themselves – and comrades – from thoughts of upcoming action and the mortal danger attached to it. Simple pranks at the expense of green recruits were common. For example, an aircraft technician might send a young assistant to the depot to fetch a 'bucket of compression', or a seasoned tanker might tell youngsters such a story:

> Once, I was sitting in my tank, the crews were at rest. I got a radio message that infantry had gone on to the attack and needed fire support. I shot, then noticed my tank move forward. Nobody's touching pedals, but the tank is advancing! Then I understood. It turned out the shell had stuck in the gun barrel, and its power was huge, you know, so it pulled the gun forward and the whole tank followed!

Thus, good story-tellers – capable of retelling previously read books, fictional or real-life stories – were popular and gained a significant audience.

Of course, people also wrote letters home to their kinfolk and families. Back then, girls sent 'triangulars' [named after the triangular-shaped envelope – trans.] to the front,

The crew of an M4A2 Sherman tank during a rest. In the hands of one crewman is an accordion – one of the most popular musical instruments of that time.

An accordion-player.

addressed 'To a Fighting Man of the Red Army', and sometimes containing a photo. Soldiers would reply to girls they liked, a correspondence would commence, and sometimes developed into a more serious relationship.

Games, such as chess, were played, and musicians – especially accordion-players – were highly regarded. That said, Meir Toker, a signalman, remembers:

> There were chess sets and several packs of captured German playing cards in the platoon. But we liked to turn on the two-way [radio] and listen to dogfights – how the opposing pilots cursed each other in the skies! People didn't have many cultural demands at the front line. We didn't see books and didn't look for them. We lived one day at a time . . .

Sometimes, a mobile cinema booth came around and units watched movies in turn. These were usually propaganda movies, so-called 'front-line film collections', in which the chief characters easily defeated whole units of stupid and comical 'Fritzes'.

From the beginning of the war, so-called 'concert brigades' were raised in theatres across the USSR. They would go to the front to perform plays or concerts. Of course, the actors were not allowed at the 'sharp end', but they did perform in the rear, some 10–30 kilometres from the front. A signaller, Olga Zonova, recalls:

> Actors from Moscow would come around [. . .] Say we came from a night shift – in an hour or two they would wake us up and we walked to watch the show with our eyes shut.

But, more frequently, front-line personnel went without such luxuries. Nurse Vera Kirichenko remembers:

> What leisure? Of dancing or entertainment parties, we had none of those. Nobody visited us. The hospital was small, no artists came to our place.

Soldiers listen to a gramophone. The photographer took some pains to make this photo an idealized scene: a chessboard, a gramophone and, of course, the main Soviet newspaper, *Pravda* ('The Truth').

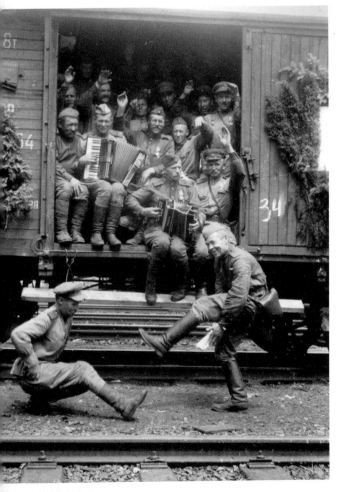

Dancing to the accompaniment of an accordion. The soldiers return home from war with combat medals and orders on their chests.

A gramophone was a real rarity on the front line. For many soldiers, hearing the voice of a pre-war singer was like a short trip home.

Pilots sing 'chastushkas' – pithy, often bawdy rhyming couplets. In the background technicians prepare a MiG-3 fighter for flight. Because of the black mount of the star on the wing, we can suppose the photo was taken not later than 1943, when compulsory white mounts were introduced in the Air Force.

Wounded soldiers convalescing. The walking wounded were lucky, they could play billiards. The less fortunate had to be content with playing draughts or dominoes.

Naval infantrymen during a rest. On the peakless cap of the rightmost soldier you can see an inscription, 'Shaumyan'. The destroyer *Shaumyan* ran aground in 1942 and its crew were sent to an infantry brigade. The soldier is armed with a PPSh submachine-gun with box magazine. An RPG-40 anti-tank grenade is in front of him. The winding of machine-gun belts round the chest has no practical purpose, but it was fashionable to emulate a trend begun in 1917 by revolutionary sailors.

Amateurs' performance. In every unit, groups of amateur performers sprang up to mark celebrations with singing and dancing.

Due to the official prohibition of card games, dominoes were popular at the front. Judging by the many decorations on the chests of some soldiers in this photo, we can assume the domino-players are from a reconnaissance unit.

A game of chess between a senior lieutenant and another fighter pilot. A Lend-Lease P-40 Tomahawk can be seen in the background.

Actors play a typical comical scene about Germans stealing women's underwear. It is interesting that the officer's awards date back to the First World War.

When a unit was withdrawn for reorganization, commanders did much to vary the soldiers' leisure time. In particular, they organized comical sporting games. In this photo can be seen a fight with sacks stuffed with rags. Opponents must knock each other down from the balance beam.

An improvised French wrestling contest.

Naval infantrymen, withdrawn from the front for reorganization, are playing volleyball during a lull in the fighting. The photo was probably taken in the Polar Regions.

An acrobatic demonstration on a Lend-Lease Willys jeep, performed by an actor of a front-line concert team.

Lidya Ruslanova sings Russian folk songs for Red Army soldiers. She uses an ordinary lorry as a stage. In the background can be seen a composite quad anti-aircraft machine gun.

A concert during celebrations for the twentieth anniversary of the foundation of the 29th Guards Red Banner rifle division (former 32nd Red Banner rifle division).

Sometimes, actors of front-line concert teams had to get to their concerts in such a way!

A film show with a portable film projector.

The sculptor, Pershudchev, creates a likeness of the female scout, Lyubov Kartseva, later killed in action.

Chapter 5
Food

To have a good meal, to drink the authorized 100 grams of vodka, to have a smoke and a long sleep – a soldier's wish list. But these simple pleasures were often elusive. The food supplied to Red Army soldiers was strictly rationed and depended on whether a unit was in the rear or on the front line. The 'cadet' and 'flyer' rations were the most nutritious, followed by those for front-line soldiers. But it was not always possible to observe these norms. This is how infantryman, Alexander Rogachev, remembers the situation at the front in the winter of 1941:

> Food rarely reached us on the front line – one day we'd be too far from the field kitchens, another we'd be pinned down by enemy fire and there was no chance to reach us. The kitchen guys would crawl out to us with thermos flasks, until we were pulled out of the attack [...] Once, a *starshina* crawled up to us: 'Soldiers, tucker time.' There were peas with meat in the thermos – but you couldn't stick your spoon in, as it was all frozen. We weren't going to light a fire for cooking, so we ate the stuff cold. And so, on the front line, we might eat once a day – mostly we lived on dry tack. We were given only three crackers and five pieces of sugar a day! We would butcher dead horses with our digging tools.

During these periods of starvation, bread was issued – one loaf between six or seven men. The bread would be cut into more or less equal parts; then, a soldier would turn his head

Cooking a dinner in field conditions. In the background you can see a stranded transport column (consisting of captured Renault, GAZ-AA, GAZ-MM trucks) being rescued by an S-65 'Stalinets' tractor (Ukraine, spring 1944).

A 'picnic' near the front line. You can see a German rifle bayonet on the belt of the Red Army soldier on the left. His commander – or maybe his commissar – on the right squats down, and you can see a gas mask jutting out of his bag. There are no weapons nearby, so we can suppose they feel out of danger.

away while another, pointing at one of the pieces, would ask: 'Who's it for?' The first soldier would name a comrade and the piece of bread found its owner. Judging from veterans' recollections, everyone dreamed of getting the top crust, as it was reckoned to be more filling.

Of course, such situations were typical of the years 1941–1942, when the Red Army was on the retreat and losing territory with its stocks of provisions. But irregularities concerning food supply also occurred later. A signalman, Meir Toker, recalls:

> Up until the summer of 1944 we'd been fed poorly. If a horse had been killed somewhere nearby it would be an instant feast for us – meat! A simple soldier always thinks where to procure something to eat. Trench life itself makes him crafty. Say there is debris of a shot-down plane nearby. You make a pretty *finka* [i.e. a Finnish knife – trans.] from the fuselage boarding and swap it for food with the cook. We would also steal. Once, we pinched a crate containing tinned food from the divisional food store and fed our whole platoon. Even now I am not ashamed of that! Only those who have experienced starvation know how hard it is to endure . . .

During advances, soldiers managed to 'liberate' foodstuffs which were considered most valuable. Dmitry Koryachek, crew member of an ISU-152 self-propelled gun, remembers:

> We had a crate with trophy crackers in our machine, and a bag of granulated sugar lay on the top of the turret. You get up in the morning, gobble our mess tin of sugar with crackers, and you won't feel hungry all day long.

The veterans recall with great pleasure tinned food supplied via the Lend-Lease plan. The tinned foodstuffs were known colloquially as 'the Second Front'.

Officers received additional rations. Usually, commanders of small units – such as tanks or artillery platoons – would share it between their men, but this was not customary in rifle units. A *Katyusha* Battery Commander, Pavel Gurevich, recalls:

Once a month the officers received the *narkom* ration: granulated sugar, butter, cereals, tobacco or cigarettes – 'Belomorkanal' or 'Gvardeyskie', sometimes 'Kazbek'. I would give most of my ration to the soldiers. What did I need all this food for? They needed it more – they did the physical work, carrying shells and so on.

Flyers were the most privileged servicemen with regard to food. They ate in canteens served by waitresses, and if there was no opportunity to get to a canteen between sorties, meals would be brought up to the planes. A Pe-2 bomber pilot, Elena Malyutina, remembers:

We were fed very well, but craved sweet things, so we'd consume condensed milk from our emergency kit. When the check committees found out, we were reprimanded quite harshly. We were given 100 grams of vodka after sorties but I didn't drink it. I gave it to the guys – the gunners.

The vodka ration of 100 grams a day was only issued to front-line fighting men during the cold season, and to airmen after combat sorties. A fighter pilot, Grigory Krivosheev, remembers:

There were three tables in the canteen: one for each squadron. We would come for dinner, the squadron commander would report that all were assembled, and only then could we begin the meal. A *starshina* would bring a nice decanter. If a squadron had made fifteen sorties, the decanter would contain a litre and a half of vodka. This vodka was put before the squadron commander and he would pour it into our glasses. If you

Dispensing porridge from a field kitchen. Notice the variation in ages among the soldiers.

received a full 100 grams, it meant that you'd deserved it; if a bit more, then you'd done your job superbly. But if your glass was underfilled, it meant you'd flown poorly. All this was done in silence. Everyone knew it was an assessment of his deeds over the last day.

The vodka ration was a primitive means to remove stress. Of course, those who liked booze often 'topped up' the fixed norm with trophy spirits or local *samogon* [i.e. 'moonshine' – trans.].

The situation with food supply changed when the troops entered German territory. A signalman, Solomon Frenkel, recalls:

There were staggering stocks of tucker in the cellars of abandoned German houses. There was such an assortment of foodstuffs and such amounts that we only marvelled at wiping out these dainties. Our cook, Uncle Vanya *the Tatar*, would throw whole piglets into the cauldron of the field kitchen and run after the guys begging: 'Boys, eat some! Take it!' but we would only turn up our noses.

Soldiers heat up mess tins with their dinner on the campfire (north-west of Tuapse, 1943).

Drinking tea in the trenches. Covered by the slope of a steep bank, Red Army soldiers could set the samovar to boil, undetected by German observers (Leningrad Front, 1941).

The field kitchen of a mountain rifle unit loaded onto a horse. The soldier leading the way is uniformed and equipped in typical style for Red Army mountain troops (Caucasus, 1942).

Another field kitchen. The soldier on the right wears a cloth *Budyonovka* helmet, which was withdrawn from military supplies in 1940. Thus we can date the photo to the winter of 1941/42. The following winter, *Budyonovkas* were definitely out of use.

A halt in a half-ruined house, following a successful battle. The soldier in the foreground put his SSh-36 helmet straight on his fur cap. The helmet wasn't adapted for this: in cold weather, it was usually worn with a special woollen cap comforter. On the belt of the Red Army soldier is a cartridge pouch for two RGD-33 grenades. An accordion-player sits on the windowsill (Leningrad Front, 1941).

Delivery of hot food in a captured German thermos flask.

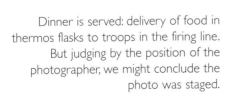

Dinner is served: delivery of food in thermos flasks to troops in the firing line. But judging by the position of the photographer, we might conclude the photo was staged.

A winter dinner: the soldiers probably had to make do with some bread with tea (Leningrad Front, 1943).

Red Army soldiers snacking on bread and tinned food in the shadow of a destroyed German motor convoy.

Dinner in the trenches. The soldier in the foreground eats with a wooden spoon, most likely home-made. Due to the abundance of SVT-40 rifles, we can conclude that this photo was taken in the rear (Kalinin Front, 1943).

Another airfield dinner (Leningrad Front, 1942).

'Asiatic hordes' – a group of soldiers, mostly from Middle Asia, warm themselves at a campfire while awaiting dinner. Notice the different styles of clothing, including overcoats, padded pea-jackets and sheepskins.

This photo was taken in a cramped dugout. One of the soldiers lights a portable stove, known as a 'Burzhuika' [a joke, meaning: 'truly bourgeois stove' – trans.], placed on a German oil can. Another soldier tries to eat, while a third proudly poses with a field telephone.

Front-line food. The photo was taken during a halt on the march. Although the soldiers' blouses are of differing patterns, this photo was taken in 1944 (3rd Ukrainian Front).

This naval gun crew receive their hot dinner while on watch. Notice the sailors eat from bowls and plates rather than mess tins.

The dinner of naval anti-aircraft gunners. One crewman doesn't stop observing the sky (Black Sea Fleet).

Crewmen of a naval aviation bomber regiment eat near their Il-4 plane, while it is refuelled. The waitress who brought the food waits till the men are finished.

These ground-attack pilots (see the Il-2 in the background) were unable to visit an airfield canteen, so dinner was served at the planes. The flyer on the right sports a raglan leather coat.

'Let's have a smoke.' A soldier lights his comrade's cigarette with a match – very valuable objects. More often, Red Army soldiers struck a spark with flint and steel or made their own lighters. On the knee of the soldier on the left, you can see a box with tobacco. The owner of the matches has a compass on his hand. On the helmet of the reading soldier, you can see a Red Star, although this was relatively rare in the fighting zone.

Another front-line cigarette break. A soldier lights a roll-up known as a 'goat's leg', due to its shape.

A typical scene during the final days of the war in Germany. The tankmen no longer fear enemy attacks and drink some alcohol, perhaps commemorating fallen comrades. They also sing their favourite songs to an accordion accompaniment.

The crew of a T-34–76 tank at dinner.

To all appearances these Red Army soldiers met either to celebrate New Year's Eve or to down their vodka ration.

Chapter 6
Sleeping

War is not only about combat but, as sapper Ivan Pyanykh observed, 'dangerous and exhausting daily work'. Under these circumstances, the opportunity to rest, to sleep, was one of the few joys in a soldier's life. Marches undertaken at night (for the sake of secrecy) were most exhausting. An infantryman, Boris Ovetsky, remembers:

> Despite some opportunities to have a snooze during the day, the desire to sleep at night was unbearable, and we learned to sleep on the move. The most important thing was to have something to hold on to – a cart, a cannon – this way you could stay asleep for a while.

If men had to rest at night they tried to stay in villages, where locals would billet the combatants. Even then, as most veterans remember, they wouldn't remove their clothes if near the front line. A sniper, Claudia Kalougina, remembers:

> Once we stayed overnight in a completely empty village house. Everyone settled quickly and I had no room at all. There was a trough for cabbage-chopping on the floor and I found my place in it. It was not comfortable, I couldn't fall asleep, but wanted to

These soldiers decided to rest near either the T-70 tank or the SU-76 self-propelled gun. If they weren't members of the crew, it was very dangerous to sleep so near to an armoured fighting vehicle (1943).

Young Kazakh soldiers sleep like the dead at the bottom of a trench. Judging by the fact they are loaded with accoutrements and their machine gun isn't established properly, we can suppose the photo was taken on the march.

sleep one way or another. In the morning, one soldier got up early and I sneaked into his place. I had a few nods of sleep and then the reveille came.

But frequently, soldiers had to sleep in the open air. While not a problem in summer, in autumn and in winter conditions were appalling, with soldiers sleeping in snow or mud. Usually, soldiers slept in pairs. Twigs or branches would be laid on the snow, one trench coat would serve as a mattress, the other as a blanket. Tank crews were a bit better off – they always had a roof over their heads. A chief of staff of a tank battalion, Konstantin Shipov, recalls:

There was little time for sleeping – it would be already 1 or 2 a.m. before you organized repairs, messed, posted sentries. And at four or five in the morning it would be time to get up. That was why we often had to sleep in the tanks: the driver and radio-operator would sleep in their seats, the gun-loader and gun-layer on the ammo stock. I – for I am a short one – would lift the gun, put the ammo stock lids on the breech end, and settle with my feet stuck into the turret niche.

Of course the rear units and servicemen from aviation units who lived in relative comfort rarely experienced difficulties of this kind . . .

Artillerymen sleep during breaks between fighting. Each member of the gun crew fell asleep at his place according to the quarter bill (Central Front, 1943).

A machine-gunner sleeps near his weapon – a Maxim model 1940 with a broad mouth, through which it was possible to fill the water-cooling jacket with snow (Central Front).

A 120mm mortar crew sleeps (Central Front, 1943).

A sleeping Red Army soldier uses a tinned food box for a pillow (Karelian Isthmus, 1944).

Chapter 7
Preparing for Combat

It's not often that an ordinary infantryman or a tank commander can recall at which village, town or city a particular action took place. Platoon Commander Vasily Bryukhov observes:

> Nowadays, it's astounding to hear some people readily recall the names of settlements near which they fought. How do I remember these names?! After the war, having toured the battlefields, I recalled this Malye [i.e. smaller – trans.] Mayachky *sovkhoz* [state-owned collective farm – trans.], named after Voroshilov. But could I remember them during the war? You get a task: 'Move between landmarks one and three.' And off you go – you look for targets, you shoot.

Only many years after the war (between 1965 and 1975) when several hundred memoirs – mostly written by senior commanders – began to be published, and reunions of veterans began to be run annually, did details of battles get connected with dates and geographical names.

A captain assigns his soldiers to their posts. Soldiers armed with PPSh submachine-guns wearing winter overalls and *valenki* felt boots.

Guards captain V. Volkov sets a task to IS-2 crews. Because of the white stripes on the tanks we can presume the photo was taken in Berlin or in the city's suburbs after the battle for the city had ended.

A rifle regiment commander shows his battalion commanders the target of attack on the map.

Senior Lieutenant Gnadenberg of the 24th Tank Brigade familiarizes the crew of a KV-1 tank with the combat area.

Commanders reconnoitre the locality. The major on the right wears a wristwatch – considered a luxury item in the pre-war USSR.

A battery commander chooses on a new map positions for a 45mm AT gun. These guns, which were designed to fire over an open sight among their crews, received the nickname: 'Farewell Motherland'.

Fighter pilots receive their combat task. The commander outlines possible manoeuvres in the sand. In the background stand British 'Hurricane' fighters, supplied to the USSR.

Chapter 8
Supplying the Front Line

The battle efficiency of any army depends on the timely supply of ammunition, arms and fuel. However, during the early stages of the war, the Soviet Union didn't possess enough *matériel* to supply an army of millions. Furthermore, support services were often incapable of running supplies amid the chaos of constant retreat. As a result, Soviet soldiers had to go into combat without adequate supplies of weapons and ammunition. A signaller, Fedor Mishurov, remembers:

> The early period of the war was a time of agonizing and humiliating retreat of the Soviet Army. The Germans had enormous superiority. Our supply was meagre: hardly any submachine-guns, only rifles and hand grenades. And we were on the retreat – over and over again [. . .] Our powerlessness and anger were especially strong under the attacks of enemy bombers, such as the Ju-87 and Ju-88. It was impossible to shoot them down from the ground.

Transportation of T-40 tanks to the front line via rail. Due to the lack of paved roads, railways were vital for supplies.

ZIS-5 trucks deliver shells to a battery of F-22 USV 76mm guns (1943).

Nevertheless, the Soviet Command always tried to maintain the ammo supply at a more or less satisfactory level, and only during the first months of the war did serious problems occur. An artilleryman, Ivan Pashkov, recalls:

> Generally speaking, we were always supplied with ammo at a normal level, and only in 1941 was the situation somewhat worse. And – just in case supplies didn't get through – we'd limit our fire rate and leave maybe a third of available ammo as a reserve stock.

Delivery of arms and ammo to fighting units was conducted mostly by trucks like the ZIS-5 and ZIS-6. The ZIS-5 had a carrying capacity of 3 tons but frequently carried up to one and a half times more. And during the slushy season or 'rasputitsa', when roads were often impassable, horses were used for logistics.

Throughout the war, supplying armour and aviation units with fuel and lubricants never caused complaints, except for some rare instances. A fighter pilot, Anatoly Bordun, remembers:

> Petrol was dispatched to our unit in special fuel trucks. Only once, at Opolje – after the battle for Warsaw – did we run out of petrol due to the *rasputitsa*, as railroad connections in that area hadn't been restored. But we were required to fly reconnaissance missions and cover important objectives at that time. That was why

they delivered us fuel in Li-2 planes. It happened like this a couple of times, and then routine supplies were established.

But at the beginning of the war supply of uniforms left much to be desired. The huge army was even short of footwear. Often the infantrymen had shoes with puttees instead of jackboots. A machine-gunner, Vasily Gordov, remembers:

> We were short of jackboots, and even as an officer, I wore boots and puttees. And this is what the puttees were like – a grey band of rough fabric, 3 metres long and 10 centimetres wide. This band overlaps a common boot and then you wrap your legs with it up to the knees, tying it up just below the knee. As a result the boots do not turn into jackboots, but warm you up better anyway, and there's less water dripping into the boots.

Only airmen and scouts were well supplied with uniforms during the initial period of the war. A scout, Leonty Brandt, remembers:

> There's no denying, the scouts were in the most privileged situation. We were even called 'the military aristocracy'. We had the best arms and were supplied at the highest level.

Nevertheless, the military supply had gradually improved during the second half of the war. When the Red Army switched to the advance, soldiers had fewer problems with provisions from the rear. Even female troops could now expect to be issued with uniforms of the required size – a rarity over the previous years. A motor specialist, Antonina Andryanova, recalls:

> It was cold in the winter. The motorists were issued with *valenki* [i.e. felt boots – trans.], and airmen and navigators had fur-lined jackboots. All *valenki* were too big for me and a sergeant said that he had small jackboots in stock, but would only give them to me with the commander's permission. I got them and began to walk about, dressed in a winter jacket and fur-lined jackboots, and since, in our garrison, nobody knew me apart from those who served in our squadron, everyone below officer rank would salute me!

Typical condition of front-line roads. A convoy of ZIS-5 3-ton trucks forces its way along a beaten rut through a sea of mud. There is a Soviet 'Emka' (GAZ-M1) passenger car in the rear of the first truck. The 'Emka' simply couldn't move through such a quagmire. On the rear wheel of the truck in the foreground you can see a chain, which, in principle, slightly increased its cross-country capability.

Soldiers unload ammunition delivered to a rifle unit. Notice the individual trench for prone firing on the right. The photo was taken in the early days of the war, since the man on the cart is wearing the SSh-36 helmet, while the man with the box is wearing the SSh-40 helmet.

The Red Army often used ordinary carts to deliver ammunition to the front line. Judging by the motley appearance of these horse-drawn vehicles, we can presume they were commandeered from civilians (1944).

Terrain was frequently so waterlogged that a horse couldn't even pull an unloaded cart by itself.

Transportation via narrow-gauge railway. An ordinary horse is harnessed either to a light cart or a broken railway handcar (Western Front, 1942).

Transportation via camels. These 'ships of the desert' were widely used by the Red Army in the steppes (Stalingrad Front, 1942).

Red Army soldiers had to drag loads over frozen rivers and lakes on home-made sledges.

Unloading supply containers from an Li-2 transport plane (1944).

Loading a Po-2 plane. While the pilot and his helpers hang tarpaulin containers with some belongings under the plane's wings, Red Army soldiers put boxes with ammunition on the passenger's seat. Obviously, the pilot will fly alone. Most likely he will deliver his load to partisans (November, 1943).

Chapter 9
Weapons Maintenance

Looking after firearms at the front line required the utmost care – after all, a fighting man's life depended on it. Machine-gunner Vladimir Ilyashenko remembers:

> We took special care over weapon-cleaning. A rifle, a tommy gun, a machine gun would be polished to a lustre, first with alkali, then with dry rags, and only then would it be greased with oil. A commander would check up before greasing, wipe the barrel with a clean white rag, and if there was a trace of anything on it he would make you clean it again.

Crews of tanks, self-propelled guns and artillery pieces had many difficulties. A T-34 tanker, Nikolay Alexandrov, recalls:

> After a march we had to service the machine – to examine the running gear, rollers, lubricate them with gun-oil, grease it up. The crewmen did it: gun-loader with the commander would do the gun, the mechanic minded his own business – regulating of the engine, brake shoes, checking the clutch to make sure it worked OK. Tank commanders, platoon commanders, company commanders all worked. The gun-cleaning was special. It had to be cleaned, then swabbed with a cleaning rod to get rid of the cupriferous stuff (leftovers of copper from shell collars). A wooden pig was

Machine-gunners clean their DP-27.

If possible, Red Army soldiers cleaned their submachine-guns while listening to the gramophone.

wrapped with rags and thick paper. The whole crew would hammer this wad – which was packed as tightly as possible in the barrel – with a rod, to get it through [i.e. in order to clean the barrel – trans.].

Everyone – without exception – envied the airmen, who not only lived in relatively comfortable conditions but also had technicians to prepare planes for sorties. Armament mechanics in aviation units were mostly girls but they were accountable on a par with men. A Junior Aviation Specialist, Nina Kounitsina, remembers:

My commander's cannon had failed during a dogfight. Fortunately this airman stayed alive! He reported to his commander that the cannon had failed due to the Junior Aviation Specialist. And that was it! The regimental commander announced in front of the formation: 'To be court-martialled.' I was in terrible grief! But I was lucky as, in two days, the squadron engineer managed to prove it wasn't my fault, and that the cartridge belt had cocked because of overloading.

'Did you clean your weapon?' It was no mere chance that such a slogan was hanging at the entrance to a dugout. Commanders had to literally train a considerable number of semi-literate Red Army soldiers, especially men from Central Asia, to clean their rifles and submachine-guns regularly.

Loading of the aircraft gun. You can see a female sergeant as the armament mechanic.

Technicians carry out full disassembling and cleaning of an aircraft's machine gun.

Air Force technicians carrying out prophylactic work on a 'Yak' fighter.

Servicing the engine of a Pe-2 dive-bomber in winter.

A shoemaker finishing a new boot tree.

Shoemakers in a field workshop repair threadbare boots. In the foreground you can see officers' boots and ordinary soldiers' kersey boots.

Chapter 10
Letters Home and to the Front

The war had ruined ordinary life for all people – more than 30 million men and women were called to the colours, millions more were evacuated. Only the mail service might help the people of this vast country to not lose each other. Indeed, for the soldiers, the mail service became the thread that linked them with their past, giving them hope for the future. Consequently, as the volume of correspondence increased, there was a shortage of envelopes and postcards. And so, from 1942, so-called 'triangulars' began to come from the front line – sheets of paper, folded in a special way, with the message on the inside and the address on the outside. Letters from the front were routed as follows: a postal unit collected envelopes, 'triangulars' or postcards from a makeshift mailbox, or directly from the soldiers themselves. The collected messages would then be taken to a field post office, wherein they would be date-stamped and packed into bags, which would be sent to a field mail depot. From there the correspondence would go in railroad wagons to all corners of the country. The examination of correspondence by military censors at the field post offices was an integral part of mail processing. Letters containing descriptions of suffering or critical comments would not be forwarded, and political officers would then run an educational conversation with their authors. Sentences containing information on unit numbers and names of settlements were meticulously crossed out. Of course, soldiers invented many methods to let their kinfolk know where they were. A scout, Vladimir Boukhenko, remembers:

My elder brother had graduated from an artillery school and met the war as a lieutenant in Moldavia. We corresponded with him on a regular basis, but hadn't seen each other since 1939. Of course, we pretty much wanted to see each other, but how could we know where our units were in action? After all, the censors had been deleting any geographical names. Then he'd set such a puzzle for me in his letter: 'We are now near the city with a name whose first part is loved by half the world, and whose second

An answer to a letter from home.

part by the whole world.' We guessed that it was Kherson ['kher' – a slang word for 'penis' and 'son', meaning 'sleep' – trans.] [...] Thus we understood that we were fighting not far from each other. Then I wrote him in the next letter: 'Our Mum lives on the same street, but in block 8, apartment 27,' and in the next letter explained that the block number was the Army number, and the apartment number the Division number.

Letters from girls, addressed 'To a Soldier of the Red Army' often arrived at the front, sometimes containing photos. A tank platoon commander, Vasily Bryukhov, remembers:

Since people were barely literate back then, tank crewmen asked me to write letters for them. I never refused and enthusiastically described the real and imaginary feats of a hero: 'I am sitting and writing to you, and imagining how beautiful you are – as the goggles of my gas mask are lit by a flare.' Of course, with my transfer to another platoon or company such correspondence quickly ceased.

In 1942 an infantryman, Semyon Kogan, received a small parcel:

There was a small tobacco pouch with an embroidered inscription: 'To a dear fighting man of the Red Army', a pair of warm wool socks and a letter: 'Hello, Comrade Kogan! I don't know your first name and therefore address you somewhat officially. On top of that I don't know you in person. But I know only one thing, that you fight against German Fascism, that you stand for our happiness, our freedom! And I decided to write you – a fighting man of our Motherland! My greetings may reach you when you are in combat, but having come out of it you will read it and remember us girls, who don't forget for a second about our dear frontliners. Be aware that our every step, our every thought are linked with you fighting comrades. And for now I am sending you a warm greeting and expect a reply. Signed: Taya Shitzgal.' Then not only I, but several other men, wrote her letters. We understood that her letter, the pouch and the warm socks were not only for me – that was a gift for all of us frontliners. I've kept this letter all my life, sixty-six years so far.

At the end of the war a different kind of correspondence began to arrive on the home front – parcels containing war trophies. Soldiers were allowed to send 5 kilograms a month, officers 10 kilograms. Commonly, clothes, lengths of fabric or leather and footwear were sent – stuff the ruined country was short of. An artillery scout, Lev Shamis, remembers:

Soldiers were allowed to send home 5-kilo parcels, and I sent only two of these. One arrived home, but in the other one, someone had replaced all my stuff with threadbare rags . . .

A Red Army soldier writes a letter sitting in his slit trench. In front of him, two F-I 'Limonka' hand grenades.

Hand-postmarking of letters at the field post office (Western Front, 1942).

Mail collection. Judging by the inscription on the letterbox – 'KFSSR, v. Uhta, 13' – we can suppose the photo was taken at the Karelian Front. It seems that soldiers took the letterbox with them and used it on the front line for collection of letters.

A postman brings letters to a rifle unit.

Reading letters from home was often the only possible way for soldiers to have some amusement.

Chapter 11
Political Work and Propaganda

The institution of military commissars was introduced into the Red Army at the beginning of the Civil War. Thousands of men from the imperial officer corps had been drafted into the Red Army and commissars were appointed to keep them in line. Commissars were given great powers, controlling each step of the commanders, whose orders were only validated by a commissar's signature. Commissars were, therefore, ultimately responsible for the actions of the commanders. They were also responsible for promotions and staff appointments. And they reported everything to the higher echelons of command. After the Civil War the official standing of the commissars changed. The new People's Commissar of Military and Naval Affairs, M.V. Frunze, favoured undivided authority. During a period of military reform, the position of commissar was abolished in those units under the charge of a member of the Communist Party. Thus the commander would, in effect, be the commissar himself, aided by a political assistant, known as a 'pompolit'. Meanwhile, commissars proper worked with non-party commanders, who remained under their jurisdiction. Later, in 1937,

The crew of an armoured train enjoy free time. While several Red Army soldiers enthusiastically follow the chess duel, a soldier in the foreground finds a place to read the newspaper, *Krasnaya Zvezda* [i.e. *The Red Star* – trans.].

the role of commissar was fully restored and they regained power over all large military formations. Smaller units – such as battalions – were overseen by 'political officers' known as 'politruks'.

In 1940 commissars were fully abolished and replaced by 'pompolits'. But the defeats of summer 1941 prompted the government to reinstate commissars yet again. They finally became history in the autumn of 1942, when the concept of 'undivided authority' was introduced for good. Then commissars became 'zampolits' [deputies performing political work – trans.] and were awarded officer status. The duties of a 'zampolit' were generally the same as those of a commissar, but their powers were greatly reduced. Basically, a 'zampolit' was simply one of a commander's deputies and was subordinate to him. As the soldiers joked: 'There is only one difference between a commissar and a *zampolit*. The commissar says: "Follow me!" The *zampolit* says: "Follow my orders!"'

There is no common opinion of the role of political officers during the war. Semyon Chervyakov remembers:

> Their duty was to explain, to support, to encourage. Good political officers sowed kind seeds in one's soul. I knew two political officers in the ground-attack aviation regiment in which I served at the end of the war: I recall only bad things about the first one, but I was prepared to follow the other anywhere, even to hell.

So attitudes varied depending on the individual. Often the most educated and sensible men were promoted as political officers. A gun-layer of a flak gun, Gennady Schutz, remembers:

> When the regimental Komsomol leader was wounded the political department appointed me as his successor. During leisure time I visited batteries, told men about the situation at the front, about the actions of the Allies. The men were mostly illiterate, after all – there were only two men with secondary education in the whole battery, the rest had between four and seven years of schooling. Of course, I had to converse with them. The Germans ran their propaganda work as well.

Certainly, the political officers carried out supervisory functions apart from the explanatory work, frequently impeding the combat control exercised by commanders. Nevertheless, it was the political officers who served as examples for the fighting men, and who took charge when commanders were killed.

A howitzer crew reads the leading article of the latest Red Army newspaper, *V boy za Rodinu* [i.e. 'Fight for the Motherland' – trans.]. This newspaper was an organ of the political department of 20th Army or 243rd Rifle Division. The photo may have been taken in 1942 in the Western sector of the front.

A political officer reads a document in front of a group of political activists. Notice the commander in the foreground, writing something in his notebook, and wearing a 'For Labour Valour' medal on his chest. It may well be that he is a literary man from the Army or Front newspaper.

Having read aloud the leading article of a newspaper, a deputy political instructor briefs a unit on the current situation.

Reading newspapers and books in an improvised Lenin's room [i.e. a room containing propaganda material and decorated in patriotic style. Such rooms were common in the USSR in schools, factories, barracks etc. – trans.]. Many propaganda papers adorn the walls – from official directives to motivational posters.

A military journalist, Yury Ardi (who became a famous radio commentator after the war), reads the Wermacht propaganda magazine, *Signal*, in Vilnius, 1944. Considering the strict prohibition against any sort of German propaganda, he and the photographer may well have been detained by SMERSH. Fortunately for them, this photo ended up in the archives without any consequences.

Chapter 12
Personal Hygiene

Observation of the rules of personal hygiene was one of the most necessary conditions for maintaining a unit's battleworthiness. During the Great Patriotic War, the centre directing the hygiene safety of troops was created in the Main Military Sanitary Department of the Red Army. But many of its instructions existed only on paper – people couldn't care less about hygiene in real combat situations where the question of life or death was resolved on a daily basis. Only when soldiers were pulled out of action could they put themselves in order. A tanker, Nikolay Shishkin, remembers:

> Sometimes we wouldn't bathe for a whole month. And sometimes we would bathe every tenth day, as was appropriate. A bathhouse would be made the following way: a log cabin covered with twigs was set up in the forest. The floor was also covered with twigs. Several crewmen would go together – one guy stokes the fireplace, another chops firewood, another brings water. You come in for washing, they give you water straight away, you get soaped, they would beat you with a bundle of sticks, rub you with a bast wisp [to improve the circulation – trans.], pour water over you – sometimes icy water intentionally. Once you're washed, back to duty, other guys come over. Wonderful!

At the start of the war, almost all soldiers had lice. But by the middle of the war lice had ceased to be permanent travelmates for soldiers. Rostislav Zhidkov, a 'Katyusha' battery commander, recalls:

In winter, Red Army soldiers often had to use snow for washing.

Morning shaving of artillerymen. The commander in blue jodhpurs shaves one of his subordinates. In the foreground is a stack of rifles. In the background can be seen the camouflaged barrel of an F-22 USV gun.

An officer shaving with the aid of a compass mirror.

Soldiers wash in a small river after a long and exhausting march.

The lice were there during the first two years. I remember we used to play the 'louse game' with our daily vodka ration at stake. We took a plywood sheet with a circle drawn in the middle, the size of a 5-kopeck coin. We would pull out a louse, place it in the centre of the circle and the winner was the guy whose louse was the first to reach the edge. Here it is, just before the winning line [...] just about to walk over, but then it suddenly freezes and another louse overtakes! The loser would be squashed straight away! But the winner was marked with a chemical pencil and hidden inside a matchstick box — it was to be a race-louse now! During the latter part of the war, if a louse was found in a bathhouse the whole unit would be made to wash again. At the same time we began using soap 'K' for disinfection. The Germans used some stinky powder against lice but still got infected with them! During advances we tried to avoid sheltering in German dugouts — otherwise we'd have to get rid of lice again.

It is noteworthy that Rostislav Zhidkov served in a Guards Mortar Unit — the elite of the Red Army. The situation was often quite different in ordinary rifle units. An artillery technician, Sergey Soloviev, remembers a washday back in 1943:

We were sent to the rear in two 1½-ton trucks. While we remained in a line of vehicles, our sergeant ran up and whispered in my ear: 'Technician, the bathhouse around the corner has been heated but there are girls in it — hope they won't kick us

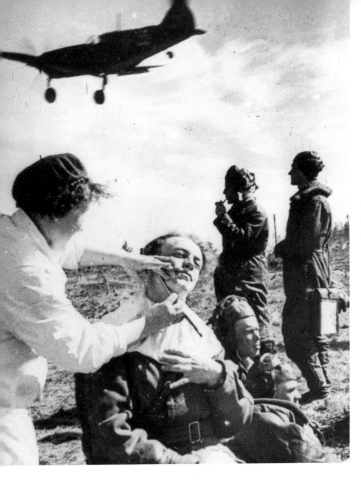

During the war, pilots had more comfortable conditions than all other arms of the service. These pilots enjoy the work of a barber girl at the airfield. Of course, they were used to the deafening sound of the LAGG-3 preparing to land.

out.' We got ready for a sudden 'assault': unwrapped our puttees, undid buttons wherever we could, and burst into the *banya* dugout, having thrown down our trench coats. Our Slavic girls began to scream, screening themselves off with washbasins somehow: 'You cheeky bastards, get out!' But having looked over our bony bodies and got an idea of our condition – in which we didn't even want to view them – they gave us a washbasin with hot water. I remember that, as I chucked my blue singlet into the hot water, it turned red straight away because of the boiled lice. Having rinsed myself somehow and thanked the kind girls, we got back to our trucks to load them just in time.

The anti-lice campaigns were run for whole units as well as individuals via the steaming of clothes. To do this, a 200-litre barrel containing water was put over a fire. Clothes were hung on crossbeams set in the barrel, which would be closed by a lid. Half an hour later, hot wet cloth would be pulled out. Another method of killing lice was to wash underwear in petrol or gas oil – a sure way to irritate the skin if the garments were not permitted to dry fully before wearing.

Shaving was performed with cut-throat razors. Often, when no mirror was available, people shaved each other. Men were only allowed to grow beards or moustaches in

After an improvised wash, a Red Army soldier sews a new undercollar to his blouse.

exceptional circumstances. As for tooth-brushing or hand-washing before eating, it may be said that these procedures were practically unknown to soldiers. Although a soldier was eligible for 150 grams of soap a month, it didn't reach the front line too often. Tooth powder wasn't available at all. It might be bought in special shops for military servicemen but the latter were rarely seen near the combat zone. The concept of toilet paper didn't exist back then. While servicemen of the rear line or Air Force units were not short of paper – present in the form of newspapers and leaflets – the front-line soldiers didn't even have this stuff . . .

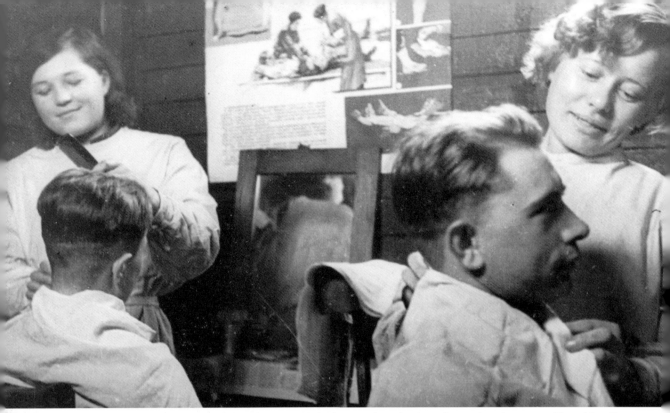

A front-line barber's shop. More likely it was stationed near a laundry battalion or headquarters. The girls will cut the soldiers' hair close to the scalp for reasons of hygiene.

During lulls in the fighting, Red Army soldiers washed without fail. This improvised bathhouse is organized in a dugout. Clean soldiers in new underwear savour a little simple happiness.

It was almost an unrealizable dream for most Red Army soldiers to take a shower. This soldier is very lucky!

These soldiers were very lucky – they could wash in a real village bathhouse.

A unit marches to the bathhouse to the strains of an accordion. The soldiers carry clean underwear and bundles of birch twigs (used to improve circulation).

Chapter 13
Decorations

In accordance with Service Regulations, there was a complicated system of incentives for personnel. And the status of individual commanders affected how they could reward their men. For example, a section commander was entitled to announce personal gratitude to his soldiers, while a regimental commander was entitled not only to announce gratitude, but also to decorate soldiers and present a cash reward. By the end of the war, when the Red Army was advancing and liberating cities, the Supreme Commander would issue an order expressing his gratitude to the troops that had participated in a particular operation. This order would be conveyed to each combatant of a unit in the form of a personal diploma. It may be said that this was the lowermost award.

Monetary rewards were the next in the hierarchy of incentives – a fixed rate established by order of the NKO [People's Commissariat of Defence – trans.]. Thus, cash was paid out for the destruction of enemy assets: 2,000 roubles for a bomber plane, 1,500 roubles for a

A senior lieutenant is presented with the Order of the Red Star.

transport plane, 1,000 roubles for a fighter plane, 500 roubles for a tank. Completion of a certain number of combat sorties and the preparation of equipment for them was also rewarded. But to put these cash rewards in perspective, it should be stated that, on the black market, a bottle of vodka or a loaf of bread cost 600 roubles. Furthermore, cash was pretty useless for front-line troops, as they rarely got a chance to spend it. Most monetary rewards – and, indeed, monthly salaries – were kept in bank accounts or transferred to families on the home front. In the latter case, a financial document called a 'money certificate' was sent and a family member would receive the soldier's salary at the local *voenkomat* [i.e. local military administrative bureau – trans.]. That said, relatives were frequently advised to donate money to the voluntary Defence Fund.

Vacations were another incentive, but used quite rarely. When war broke out, all regular leave for military servicemen was cancelled, except for the sick or wounded. An artillery battalion commander, Petr Mikhin, who found himself on the brink of nervous exhaustion because of intense fighting for the Dnestr bridgehead in the summer of 1944, remembers:

> The Divisional Commander summoned the Rifle Battalion Commander, Morozov, and me. Having seen our condition, he ordered us both to Odessa, to a resort for officers. We had not even heard that such places existed, as it was mostly political, HQ and supply officers who stayed there. The General told us straight: 'For the first time, the division has just received two tickets for the seaside. I sacrifice them to you – only because I know you are irreplaceable combat officers.'

Government decorations were the most widespread and desirable awards. The medal 'For Combat Merit' was considered the lowermost of this kind. Frequently, officers awarded their mistresses [known as 'PPZh', meaning 'pokhodno-polevaya-zhena' – literally, 'field-marching wives' – trans.] with it and because of this it was dubbed 'For Sexual Exploits' [it sounded similar to the original name – trans.] amongst the fighting men. A female medic, Zoya Nikiforova, remembers:

> The Platoon Commander, Alexandrov, my future husband, seated me at the table in a bath-hut. He himself sat down imposingly, legs crossed, with a cigarette in his long fingers. He asked my name and where I was from: 'Do you have any awards?' – 'Yes.' – 'Which one?' – 'For Combat Merit.' – 'Aha . . .' After the war he told me the following: 'At first we thought that you'd sinned a lot and had come to our platoon to pray for forgiveness!'

The Order of the Red Banner was the highest award for combat, and soldiers and officers could be recommended for special merits to the rank of Hero of the Soviet Union. Each

A regimental or divisional commander presents a Red Army soldier with the Order of the Red Star. Notice the commander's shoulder-belt: you can clearly see a pocket for a whistle attached to the belt with a little strap.

award had its status, this or that award would be given for certain deeds in action. An artillery observer, Lev Andreev, recalls:

> We, observers, would be honoured if we spotted an enemy battery that, as a consequence, was subsequently destroyed. But there was also a clause in the regulations – 'Shooting down an enemy plane using a personal firearm' – so my mate, Roman Rybalko, decided to do this and win a decoration. There were many enemy air

Parading the divisional banner.

Mass presentation of medals 'For Bravery' or 'For Combat Merit', as well as Orders of the Red Star, following successful fighting. Most likely the photo was taken at the beginning of autumn 1941.

raids. He would choose a high spot and fire from his PPSh. I ridiculed him, having said that it was impossible to shoot down a plane with a tommy gun. Soon, a German rifle with a whole bag of armour-piercing incendiary rounds turned up in his possession, apart from the submachine-gun. He began to shoot with single shots – not bursts. Bombs are falling, all are trying to hide, praying for God's preservation, and Rybalko begins firing from his rifle next to you! Of course, everyone cursed him, but Rybalko simply moved away a bit and continued shooting. He never managed to down a plane, but by the end of the war he got his longed-for 'Glory' [i.e. the Order of Glory – an award for private soldiers – trans.].

Of course, there was no question of fairness when it came to decorations. Much depended on one's relationship with superiors. A gun commander, Grigory Sagalovich, remembers:

God knows by which routine, yardstick or criterion the decision to decorate soldiers was taken. We stuck close to each other – two guns at the Dnieper bridgehead: Filippov's and mine, shooting together, smacking onto the same targets with approximately the same efficiency. Filippov was made a Hero of the Soviet Union and given a month's leave, his crewmen all got medals. We got nothing [. . .] well, we told him: 'Lucky you, Filippov,' congratulated him, but there was no envy . . .

A signalman, Petr Semyonov, recalls:

The artillery commander of our division had his personal cook. When someone was decorated in the division he would say to the commander: 'Comrade Colonel, everyone gets decorated, but not me. But I'm in combat too.' Then the commander orders that his cook be decorated. And you know what? They recorded at HQ: 'Killed twenty Hitlerites by the fire from his submachine-gun.' They gave him the medal 'For Valour' or 'For Combat Merit'. What Hitlerites could they mean, when he never held anything in his hands but a ladle, a fork and a spoon? And those who'd gone into the attack got nothing! Why? I'll explain. Today, the section and platoon commanders get killed, tomorrow the company commanders, several days later there's no battalion commander any more. Who's gonna write a recommendation? On top of that, Komsomol leaders would say to commanders before they decorated someone: 'Don't forget my guys.' It meant that those who were not Communists or Komsomol members, or had been in occupied territory – get out of here!

Apart from that, from 1943, when the tide turned for the Soviets, more decorations were given, while, during the earlier period of retreat and heavy defensive fighting, decorations were rare. A battalion commander, Khaim Noson, remembers:

> I had filled recommendations for decoration for all the fighting men of my battalion who had distinguished themselves, but the paperwork would be lost somewhere at headquarters, and, sadly, the fortitude of ordinary private soldiers who had excelled in combat during that difficult time remained unmarked.

The war was over, and many of its participants had never been honoured. In 1985 all surviving war veterans received an Order of the Patriotic War as a memorable award. Many reckoned that the same order, won in combat conditions, had become just a memorial badge.

A private receives a qualifying badge from his commander (1943).

Decorating A-20G Boston bomber crews at an airfield. In contrast to other arms of the service, pilots were heaped with the highest awards. This Guards senior lieutenant, who receives the decoration, already has two Orders of the Red Banner. On the right of his chest there is a Guards badge.

The 65th ground-attack Regiment received 'Guards' designation and became the 17th Guards Regiment. Its commander, Colonel Belousov, takes an oath while receiving the new banner.

Colonel Belousov, commander of the 17th Guards ground-attack Regiment, fixes a new medal to a senior lieutenant's blouse.

Chapter 14
Women at the Front

After the Revolution, the Soviet State conducted a policy of involving women into socially useful work. The emancipation of women, and their entry into traditional 'masculine' trades and sports, were presented as the greatest achievement of socialism – here, real equality was manifested, as women were liberated from 'domestic slavery'.

At the start of the war, thousands of women rushed to the Army, eager not to fall behind the men, feeling that they were capable of enduring all the hardships of military service and, most of all, consolidating their right to defend the homeland with the men. These girls were prepared for courageous acts – having been raised on books full of heroism and adventure – but not for the practicalities of military service. Discipline, ill-fitting uniforms (too large by many sizes), a male environment, plus a heavy physical workload – all combined to create a harsh trial. A searchlight operator, Evdokya Kozlova, remembers:

> Initially, they gave us men's uniforms, which we would alter: we'd trim the trench coats, clip the blouses. English-made boots were too big by five sizes. There was no female underwear. We sewed bras from rags, issued to us for cleaning weapons.

I. Bondarenko and S. Miryuk volunteer for the Army.

In 1942 a special female sniper school was established near Moscow. In twenty-seven months around 2,000 women graduated. Some became very professional and highly decorated. These snipers were armed with Mosin rifles plus PU optical sights. The girl on the right is decorated with the highest military award, the Order of the Red Banner, as well as the Order of Glory 3rd Class. On her right breast is an 'Excellent Sniper' badge.

But women always had one way out – get pregnant. In this case, a woman would be discharged from the Armed Forces at the sixth month of pregnancy. An aviation technician, Nina Kounitsina, recalls:

> My dear Mum wrote to me: 'My sweet daughter, your girlfriends have come home, they will give birth to children, why do you stay there? Come home, I won't curse you for a baby.'

As for the attitude of men to the presence of women in combat, Nikolay Shishkin, a tanker, remembers:

> Our medic was Marousya Malovichka. When one of our tanks was shot up before our eyes, a crewman leaped out, but the Germans were on the spot. They snatched him and dragged him to a dugout. We watched but could do nothing about it. Then she grabbed a machine gun from an assistant – listen up, had I not seen this with my own eyes I wouldn't have believed it – but she leopard-crawled up to the German lines, shot the sentries, broke into the dugout, pulled that tanker out and walked him back to us. She was awarded with the Order of the Red Banner. We respected women of that kind. But all sorts of things were said behind their backs: 'Air raid!' or 'Rama!' [i.e. Russian nickname for the German FW-189 twin-fuselage reconnaissance plane. Basically, the

guys were saying 'Watch out!' – trans.]. What it meant was this: if there's a woman around, you got to hide. Without women around, the men felt themselves free to talk, but as soon as a woman turned up they tried to be more polite, not to swear. They ennobled us. They decided to make radio-operators and machine-gunners out of women in a neighbouring brigade. This idea lasted for a couple of weeks – it's not a female business to fight.

Often, women themselves gave grounds for gossip and anecdotes, having become one of those who were dubbed, contemptuously, a 'field-marching wife'. Nikolay Posylayev recalls:

As a rule, women who'd found themselves at the front soon became officers' lovers. There was no other way. If a woman was alone, there would be no end of harassment. But it was a different story if she was with someone [. . .] However, the most sincere love occurred on the front line too. It was tragic, for it had no future – death separated lovers far too often. But love is strong, it made people live and dream of happiness, even under fire.

I want to conclude with the words of a mortar crewman, Vladimir Logachev, who was badly wounded in the spring of 1943:

Wounded men were washed straight after arrival in the Ufa hospital. This procedure was run the following way: ten strong girls, being completely naked – only in small oilcloth aprons – washed the trench dirt off the wounded men in a well-heated room, cutting off old bandages and cleaning wounds. I passed into the possession of a young, dark-haired Ukrainian girl called Oxana – I can see her now as before. Yet I don't know if this procedure had been worked out intentionally or not, but the young hot bodies of these girls, their tender hands, revived many a wounded man's will to live . . .

Radio-operator of an artillery unit, A. Ivakhina, with RBM radio set. The girl is decorated with a medal and a badge, 'Excellent Signaller' (1944).

Il-2 'Shturmovik' reargunner, R. Koriagina. This photo was probably staged or taken after a sortie, since flyers were extremely superstitious and would not allow photos before a mission (1943).

Armament mechanic, M. Khlomova (1943).

The inscription under this photo says: 'Brigade commander Comrade Sytnik after the concert.' Pictured near the military man is an actress of a front-line concert team, judging by her civilian dress.

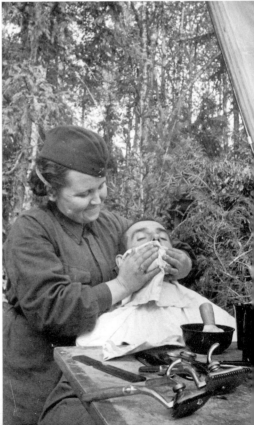

Shaving an officer in a laundry platoon or at an HQ barber's shop. Such a service was practically inaccessible for ordinary Red Army soldiers.

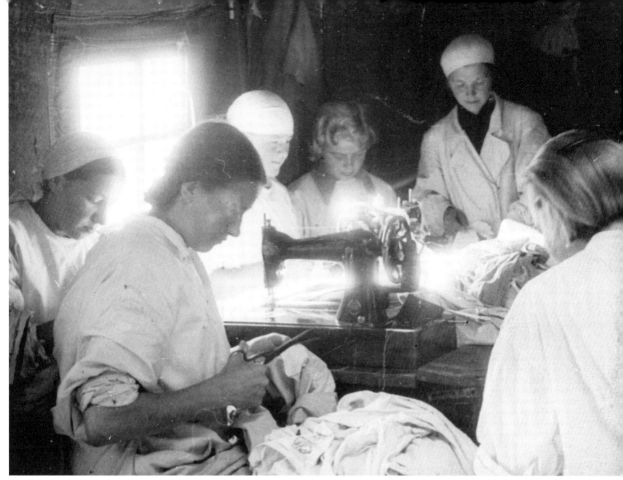

In this photo you can see, most likely, darning of soldiers' underwear in a laundry battalion. But it's also possible the girls in the photo are medical orderlies of a medical and sanitary battalion making bandages out of old underwear. There is a Singer sewing machine on the table – such machines were produced at the beginning of the twentieth century in Podolsk.

Ironing clean underwear in a laundry battalion. Due to the absence of electricity in field conditions, girls had to make do with very heavy coal irons.

A female traffic controller on one of the military roads. To her left is a German Hetzer tank destroyer, put out of action or abandoned by its crew. The traffic controller – armed with a Sudaev submachine-gun – lets a 'Studebaker', towing a ZIS-3 76mm gun, pass through. The soldiers in the truck are obviously shouting jokes and inviting the girl to have a ride with them.

Awarding soldiers with medals. In the photo, the major of artillery carefully adjusts the new medal on the soldier-girl's blouse.

Chapter 15
Medical Services

As the infantrymen used to say at the front: 'We don't have much choice: sooner or later the *Narkomzem* [literally, "People's Commissariat of Agriculture" but this acronym was used as a pseudonym for hell – trans.] or the *Narkomzdrav* [People's Commissariat of Health Protection – trans.] will take care of us.' But to let the *Narkomzdrav* take care of a wounded man, first he had to be evacuated from the battlefield. Riflemen were categorically banned from assisting wounded out of the combat zone – one might have been labelled a deserter, with subsequent commandeering to a penal company. Instead, evacuation was conducted by company medics. At the beginning of the war young females were drafted to fill this position, but to drag a wounded adult man from a battlefield with his firearm (salvation of a wounded man without his firearm was not considered during recommendations for decoration) was an extremely difficult task. Therefore, as a battalion medical attendant, Michael Sitnitsky, recalls:

> Sturdy mature men aged 30–35 were picked as medics. Not all set hopes upon God, but the soldiers always hoped for the battalion medics and trusted us. They knew that we would save our wounded comrades and wouldn't leave them on the battlefield to bleed to death.

Wounded men arrived at the battalion medical post, where they would get first aid. Then they would be transported to the divisional medical battalions in carts, sleighs or trucks. A medic, Nina Bobovkina, remembers:

Photographers seldom took photos of medical instructors during a real battle. But here is a rare real-life photo on this theme. Far in the background you can see a soldier firing his Sudaev submachine-gun. A wounded Red Army soldier, who receives medical help from a girl in a beret, has a PPD submachine-gun. Due to these details we can date the photo to 1942, and we also can suppose that it was photographed on the Leningrad Front.

Transportation of wounded men was a very difficult duty for girls. Six stretchers were set up at three levels on holders in specially equipped 1½-ton trucks. Five more, lightly wounded, men would be placed on a folding bench. Badly wounded men – whose coats and boots had been removed – were wrapped in special fur or wool blankets to keep them warm against the cold. A medic would have to hold back the upper and medium level stretchers to prevent the wounded from falling down due to heavy jolting. If a unit was in combat, the flow of wounded was endless.

A fighter pilot, Alexander Shavarev, who found himself in a hospital after his plane had been shot down, remembers:

Oh, I saw a lot of that! Just imagine, a surgeon covered in blood, his sleeves rolled up, and there's a big knife in his hands! He comes up to someone: 'How's it going, brother?' The guy says: 'Oh, painful.' The surgeon has a look and orders: 'Shave him up!' Done. The surgeon chops off what's necessary and chucks it into a bowl. He yells: 'Sister! Dress him up and send him off!' He does an operation, then goes to a table, gulps half a glass of spirits, and then back to work. The sisters say he's had no sleep for the second day running.

The next step was to send wounded men to a specialized evacuation hospital. Many lightly wounded men did their best to stay in the medical battalion, for it would be almost impossible for them to make it back to their units after convalescence. Having been healed, a soldier would undergo a medical examination, and if he was recognized as fit for combat, he would be commandeered to a transition point, where representatives of units and formations would come up to pick up reinforcements. Thus a soldier had a chance to change his military occupation after being wounded. An infantryman, Dmitry Markov, remembers:

Some 'buyers' from the Army came over to the transition point and said: 'We need soldiers to reinforce an artillery regiment.' I thought: 'Enough is enough. I ain't gonna join the infantry, only the artillery.' Why? For I'd done lots of marching from Kursk and almost to Kiev! There'd been a clear feeling: sooner or later you're gonna get killed or wounded . . .

Last salute at a comrade's grave. We can date the photo to the very beginning of the war because by the middle of 1942 SVT rifles were almost out of use at the front line.

Funeral of a fallen pilot. In contrast to most front-line soldiers, airmen had the questionable privilege of being buried with full military honours. The pilot's combat comrades come to pay their last tribute to him. The numerous girls in the photo are most likely airfield signallers. The boy on the right looks like a typical 'son of the regiment' of an airfield service battalion.

A senior lieutenant or a political instructor of the Red Army killed by a direct hit to his head.

Typical exterior of a soldiers' mass grave — a small pyramid with a star. After the war such improvised battle-zone memorials were found every hundred metres. Later, some of these memorials were rebuilt as real monuments, while others were broken. The soldiers' remains were carried to large military cemeteries. Sometimes, however, it was only the names from plates that were removed, and not the actual bodies of fallen soldiers.

A medical instructor bandages a soldier, who has been dragged off the battlefield. Notice that he wears the wide trousers of a camouflage uniform kit. It was more comfortable and safe to crawl in such trousers.

A staged photo used to demonstrate how crewmen pull a wounded comrade from their tank.

Transfer of wounded soldiers from a bus to a hospital train.

Military field dentistry. For many soldiers a visit to the dentist was more frightening than any battle.

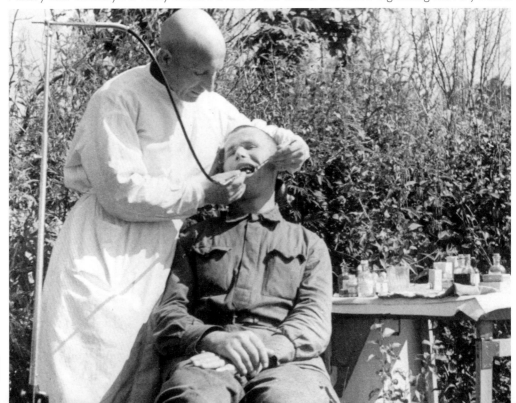

Chapter 16
Going Home

The very first feeling that engulfed everyone after the announcement of the end of hostilities was the joy of having survived. Every veteran remembers this day – 9 May 1945. For an Army driver, Lidya Gloushenko, it was like this:

> I was on sentry duty with a carbine. Suddenly, shooting broke out – shouts of 'Victory! Victory!' I threw away my carbine and rushed to my girlfriends to tell them the Victory had come. I ran up to them, we began to hug each other, to cry – and I felt that something was squelching in my jackboot. I had a look – the jackboot was full of blood. I fainted away [she had been wounded by a bullet or splinter from the improvised victory salute – trans.].

Vladimir Temerov, a Pe-2 bomber navigator, remembers the moment he found out the war was over:

> It happened, perhaps, about six in the morning. The squadron commander ran into the room shouting: 'Victory! The war is over! Get up!' He leaped out into the corridor and began to shoot the ceiling. Of course, everyone jumped out of bed, ran out onto the street and began shooting with pistols, yelling 'Hurray!' But combat sorties would go on for some more days.

When the euphoria of the first moment of peace had passed, many men began to wonder what to do next. Vasily Bryukhov, who found himself in Austria in the capacity of tank battalion commander, remembers:

> I was billeted in a house with a café on the ground floor, and on the first floor were the premises of its owner, who had fled with his family. On the morning of 9 May I

'Motherland meets her victorious sons' is written on the banner beneath the portrait of Stalin.

Senior sergeant Baranov returns to his home town, Ivanovo.

woke, swung the window open, sat on the windowsill. It was beautiful! Mountains, apple trees in blossom, green fields with crops, the sun. And I felt so sad! The war is over. What next? What can I do? Only march, build up a defence line, lead people into battle. There were no unanswered questions during the war. But what was ahead of me now? What to do? Where could I go when my house had been ruined, my family had perished or had been evacuated somewhere? Millions of people, who had to return to their pre-war occupations and rebuild the country ruined by the war, had to resolve these questions.

The victors returning from the front were received with joy – for short-handedness was everywhere. A battery commander, Alexander Rogachev, recalls:

We were received very cheerfully and treated very cordially. There was no aloofness or indifference. And we wouldn't put on airs either. Well, you've been at war and what? You've come back – now enter the peaceful life. And we'd missed it so badly! So much we wanted to study, to work. Despite all difficulties, the optimism and vivacity were always with us.

The invalids of war were worse off. Those who had lost limbs or sight had no chance to work. They lived on meagre pensions or went begging on trains. There were those who began to drink heavily on returning home. At first it was caused by the desire to have fun

We are from Berlin! Lieutenant General Telegin bids farewell to his demobilized troops, departing for the Motherland from Berlin in July 1945.

The war is over – families reunited.

and get rid of the burdens of the war, then it would become a habit. By no means was life easy for women who had returned from the front. Lidya Gloushenko, a driver, remembers:

Of course, we who had been at war were called 'frontovichki' [i.e. 'front-line' girls – trans.], which was a synonym for 'women of easy virtue'. That was why, at first, many of us were hiding the fact that we'd been at war – but not me. I had a younger sister born in 1941 and then one pesky admirer got into the habit of paying me visits. Once he asked me: 'Is this girl yours?' – I said, 'Yeah, I've brought her from the front!' I saw him no more. My Mum said, 'My God! You front-line girls are not too popular anyway and you create a scandal for yourself on top of that . . .'

Having returned from the war, people did their best to forget everything related to it as soon as possible. Olga Khod'ko remembers:

We wouldn't talk much about the war. All of us reckoned that this calamity had passed and needed to be forgotten. I remember very well that there was no such directive from above, but everyone had grown tired of the war so badly that we wanted to rid ourselves of all that was related to it.

Official propaganda extolled the role of Stalin and his generals in the war. Films were made and plays were staged in theatres about them and the abstract 'Soviet people'. The oblivion lasted for twenty years until the trauma inflicted by the war had healed over. A machine-gunner, Abram Shoikhet, remembers:

Before the war there was a soccer team in our Pervomaiskaya Street, and in a neighbouring street there was a rival team. And once we decided to get together. And when we met we were scared – only five of us were left, all invalids covered with wounds: Senya Feinberg, Yasha Kremer, Misha Fishkis, Shika Vintfeld and I [. . .] All our other mates from the two streets had died in the war. Only then did I finally become aware how ruthlessly the war had mowed my generation . . .

Kiev station in Moscow. The photo was probably taken in autumn 1945.

Demobilization continued for several years after the war ended. This photo was taken in 1948, in the 'Krasnyi boets' *kolkhoz* [collective farm – trans.], located in the Krasnodar region.